unloving the knife

unloving the knife

Lilith Kerr

Q AN IMPRINT OF QUERENCIA PRESS

ISBN 978 1 959118 22 0

www.querenciapress.com

First Published in 2023

Querencia Press, LLC
Chicago IL

Printed & Bound in the United States of America

contents

content warning

this collection contains explicit discussion or reference of:

- knives, sharp objects, and other weapons
- suicide, suicidal ideation, and self-harm
- depression, obsessive-compulsive disorder, dermatillomania, and anxiety
- blood and gore
- injury, violence, and body horror
- sexual assault and sexual harassment
- death and grief
- strong language
- internalized homophobia and homophobic slurs

ACT ONE

♥ kissing the blade ♥

unloving the boy

i'm still a child—

    all wire-strung limbs and teeth like barbed wire.

i'm still a child and i've never been kissed.

      okay, that's not quite true; there was that time in the middle of may,

    standing next to my best friend, the weight of sunlight draped across my

shoulders and pollen under my chin.

    // do you like butter? //

      but i don't count that

(because we were only nine // because it was just a dare // because her older cousin

      wanted to watch and i've never felt more like a butchery).

i'm no longer standing in that field with fistfuls of wildflowers.

but i'm still so young, and a boy is desperately in love with me,

his eyes like goblets overflowing with lust.

    // i blush at the turn of a phrase //

he trails me down the halls, drags his chair closer to mine in art class.

every word he speaks, every time i trace his gaze to my mouth, the room floods with expectation;

a wanting left hanging   untouched   and   rotting in the air.

        i don't love him.

                this unsettles me, and i don't know why.

i imagine him kissing me—

        his mouth opening wet and hot and   hungry   over mine.

i try to conjure butterflies from the pit of my gut;

                transfigure stomach acid into sparks.

        but all i feel is a nausea slithering putrid and slick up my esophagus.

last ditch efforts, and end-of-the-line fear and

                i try to sculpt my features into the image of adoration,

inject affection into my smile like botox.

instead, i do little more than lay indifference,

        antiseptic and dulling,   at his feet.

                // a gutted bird brought home by the cat //

so, i bandage his wounds and i tell myself i don't need my heart to

        eat itself alive with longing;

that the ouroboros never did itself any good in

choking to death.

but there's this   girl in my astronomy class,

and she has eyes that open like an eclipse,

and i don't understand why my heart is writhing in my chest

(because it might as well have been dead in every moment before this).

i can reason it a million different ways—keep my eyes trained on the middle distance.

// out of sight, out of mind, right? //

i can try to gorge myself on the illusion of apathy.

and maybe, in another lifetime, it could work;

i could swallow my heart and pretend to love the boy just like everyone tells me to.

but then she   grins at me, and suddenly,

i'm nine years old again, feeling the first tug of affection for a girl and tasting blood.

// feeling the sentient bite of guilt deep in my abdomen //

yet   desire   has always been unrelenting;

something so much bigger than what i can   hide away in my fists.

serendipity

the clouds didn't have to rake themselves across the horizon—

didn't have to flood the air with ozone and break the sky wide as a scream.

there's nothing in any cosmic blueprint that necessitates your existence;

nothing to guarantee you standing there without an umbrella,

drenched in rainwater and the technicolor of neon signs.

but there you were,   you, with your eyes like lightning

and your hair dripping shadows.

i'd like to think it was fate.

but maybe god thought to drop the strings for just a moment;

an architect putting down the pencil.

and maybe, in the vastness of every "perhaps",

// in the space between choice and kismet //

there exists a version of me that never met you—a version of me that stands alone in the rain:

that never even steps outside in the first place.

just know that given the chance, i'd choose to walk into that heavy bluing of a night.

i'd choose you

every   single   time.

the topography of want

there's always breath you never knew you were holding.

there's always want that sits patient,

      that stays dormant and translucent.

and then one day, you're sitting on the bus,

      or unpacking groceries,

           or perched on the kitchen counter with her hip against yours,

and she knocks the breath

                right out of your lungs.

it's the line of desire that charts a course up the ridge of your sternum.

it's finding yourself lightheaded and reeling from the most insignificant movement

of the hair, the eyes,

                the abstraction of a palm.

and there's this moment between inhale and exhale,

when your ribcage seems to crack wide open—

unspool like a ribbon onto the floor.

and you realize that you're already chest-deep and barely treading water.

    -   *this is gonna hurt, isn't it?*

witchblooded

my mother raised me in gardens, in the tangles of ravines and the hollows of oak trees,

always with one hand pressed against the sun-soaked

sanctity of earth;

a cathedral of green.

she taught me to worship women with eyes darker than obsidian,

with shoulders like altar tables and spines of anathame.

so it's no surprise i fell for a girl with a mind

like divinity, burning brighter than any flame

i've held between two hands.

she speaks with a voice like an incantation;

in her wake, the air turns to

religion.

apotheosis

i still remember that last summer:

your dark hair bleached gold

in the indelible heat,

the sun resting honeyed and full in the nimbus sky,

      kissing the slope of your throat golden.

(think apollo,

think midas running his finger down the length of your cheek

                                                bone.)

there's this inherent flush,

this raging of capillaries

every time you speak.

and so i think   i was born aching—

the way the moon aches for the dawn,

reaching with silvered fingers across an empty horizon   line.

we took our bikes out by the river and stood by the banks as i watched light   fractal and shatter across your skin.

// a kaleidoscope personified //

and every nebulous atom in my body sparked alight;

a fever blazing   ravenous   up the nape of my neck

// an arcing of electricity between synapses //

// neurons that will never not be etched with your name //

i swear, i've never felt tenderness this heavy.

i wanted to kiss you then—

you, with your eyes like suncatchers, and your mouth like god.

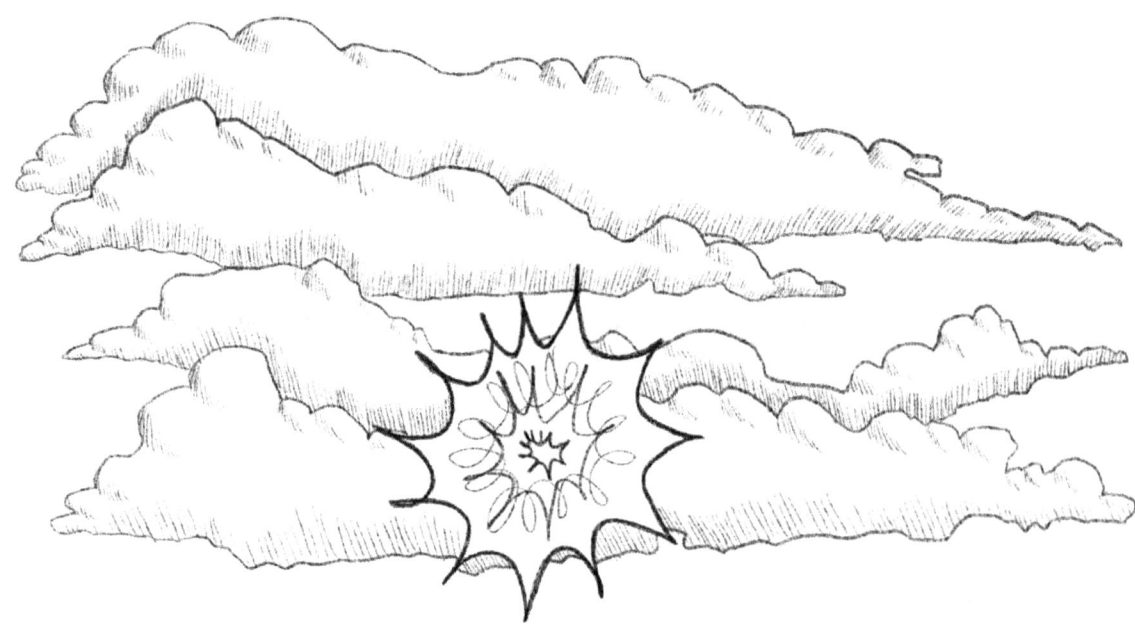

diaphanous

it's four a.m. and the moon is tangled in my bedsheets.

i'm whispering your name again like a prayer

                          into the blurring mist of early morning.

        do you feel the way my heart tugs on yours?

the way it drifts through the passersby that mark the streets with their footfalls,

        crossing the haze of high beams into the cavern of your chest?

i dream in your mother tongue,

the words coating the back of my throat like honey.

do you ever think of me in these quiet moments?

does the thought of

        my hips //

                my waist //

                        the plunge of my collarbones

tear you to shreds the same way i crumble under your gaze?

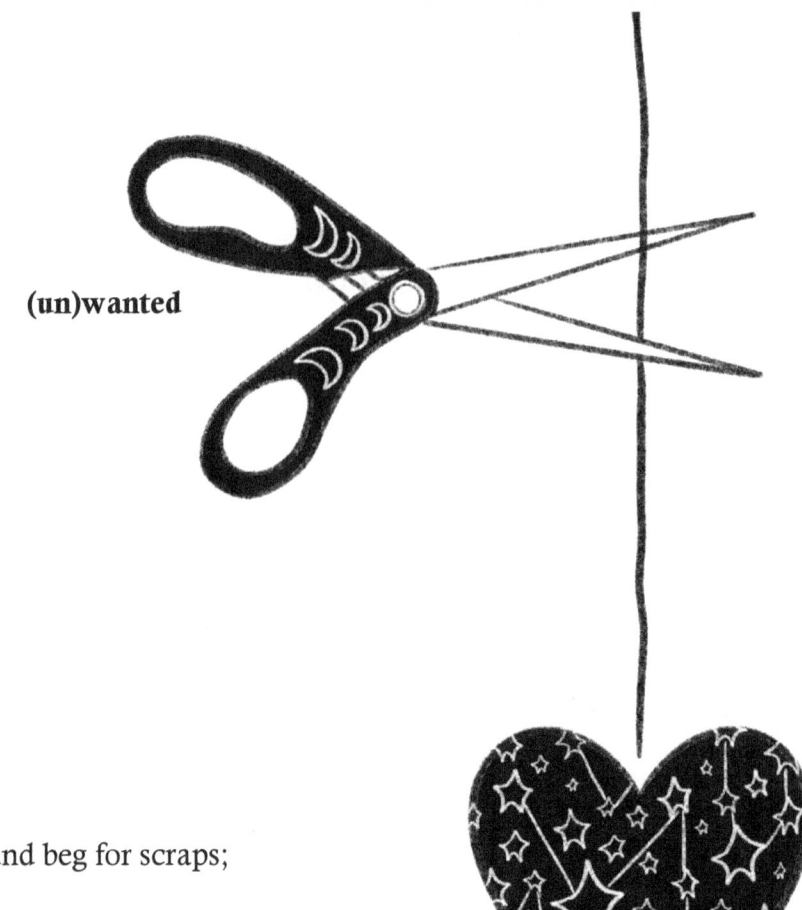

(un)wanted

call me wanted.

call me yours,

call me loved without making me sit up and beg for scraps;

  without bisecting the pulp of my chest and eating my heart bloody.

      call me worthy even when my mind tethers itself to death and breaks

     bread with the reaper.

show me i can be loved fully-clothed—take me home without undressing me,

without pressing

     my body

      against a wall and

     your hands

      between my thighs.

could you love me simply—without any strings attached?

orpheus // eurydice

souviens-moi à la face cachée de la terre;

le point cardinal est toujours

étalonné vers ton battement de cœur.

je te regarde alors que tu descends dans

l'obscurité—

une colombe encagée de sa propre

chef.

si tu me montres tes mains tendues,

je sais que je me dissoudrai en l'air lourd

de la poussière et de la lumière.

je suis désolée, ma chérie;

je crains que je sois

plus fantôme qu'humain

(des dernières lueurs dans une crypte déjà

remplie d'échos).

et nous savons tous les deux qu'il n'y a pas

de salut pour les âmes perdues.

follow me to the underbelly of the earth;

the compass point is always

calibrated to your heartbeat.

i watch you as you descend into the

darkness—

a dove caged of its own

volition.

if you show me your outstretched hands,

i know i will dissolve into air heavy

with dust and light.

i'm sorry, my dearest;

i fear i am

more phantom than human

(an afterglow in a crypt already full of

echoes).

and we both know there's

no salvation for lost souls.

killing time, killing gently

after richard siken

you're in a car next to a girl with a grin like a firecracker

and you love her the same way your body loves breath

(unconsciously // inevitably // to the end of days).

but the word "dyke", the fiction of the fanged and clawed and leering

lesbian lingers like a vaporous thing in the back of your mind; some kind

of sick poltergeist,

and   god,

wouldn't she just be disgusted if she knew you loved

her with all the gravity of a neutron star

.

of course

you can't tell her how you feel. how could you?

you can't peel your skin back

to reveal the rotted root of your heart,

pulsing gory and bludgeoned in your chest—

you can never give away exactly how deeply, gut-wrenchingly

starving you are.

so you push the hunger further down into the quietest parts of you—

you break your neck on the sharp

edge of longing

and let the steady rhythm of the car lull you to sleep.

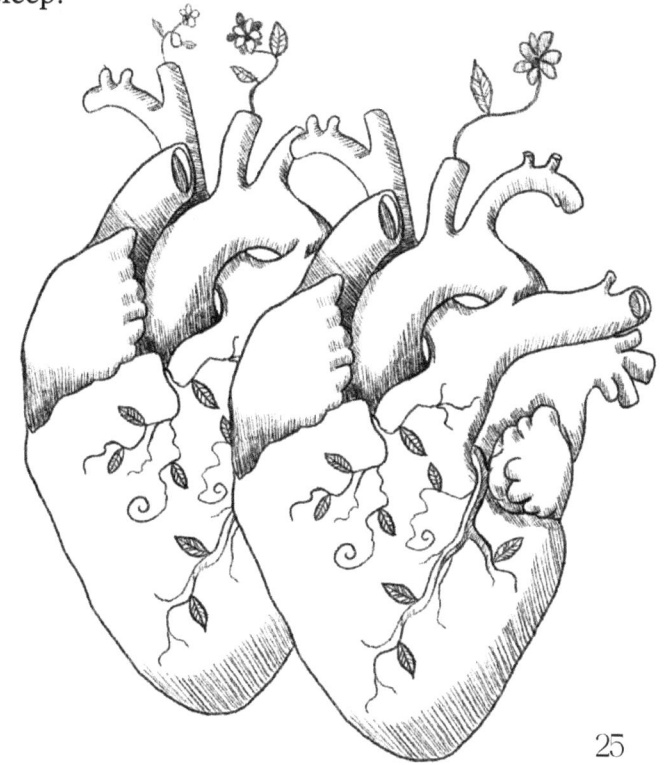

kerosene

i asked a thousand times before i even touched her,

    as though i would corrupt with nothing more than the bare heat of my skin.

        (hand in wretched hand.

            spit in my palms and i'll kiss yours.

          two girls and an eternity of friendship between them—

one scorched with fear and acting as though she feels nothing.

          the other, pretending she doesn't see it)

even now, there's an apology

sliding from under the pink of my gums like

                        some kind of invocation;

    a hymn rising in rhythm, thrumming with want.

    i'll play the supplicant swallowing matches like sacrament—

she can be the unreachable god with no need for resurrection.

      // i blaspheme with my desire //

and it's like i'm burning up from the inside out.

like i'm drunk on kerosene and ready to be set alight.

           like i'm afraid i'll burn her too.

guiltless

i don't want to be a boy,

    not really.

but i wish i could love women the way men love women—

    brazenly, with eyes facing forward.

i want to scream my adoration, hold it up to the light

    and let it refract citrine and blinding in the sharpness of morning.

            because there's a soft wonder in the way women

                spark alive in the shadows:

            the way i trembled when she took my hand in hers,

        how i covet her affection, hoard the memories of every lingering gaze,

            keep them hidden in the softened spaces

                between cartilage and sinew.

but instead, i love cautiously.

    i love quietly; second-guessing every word, every glance—

    every unspoken endearment

  rabbiting feral in my throat, catching on the hooks of my teeth.

// dissolving to dust //

the sweetest armageddon

i would know you in a crowd of millions

simply by the way your body draws breath;

the way you stand—an effigy of light set against a backdrop of stars.

i would know you even when the sun blooms hot

    and hungry

        and desolate.

i think i would know you at the edge of creation,

at the heat death of the universe.

unraveling

FADE IN

INT. HOUSE - EVENING   1

KITCHEN

We (break) open on the kitchen floor. There is a window towards the back of the room. The day is dying and we watch it dissect itself into an inferno. A woman and a half sit on the ground. Neither is holy.

UNKNOWN (V.O)

you pull yard after yard of night-drenched thread

from the trenches of my throat.

they wrap your fists up in darkness

and tangle in your lap;

a writhing, muddied swirl of tentacles.

BASEBOARDS

The corners of the room are shuddering (Was it like that before? No one can remember). It's

getting dark outside and the air is somehow thicker than it was before. Heavier, too.

UNKNOWN (V.O)

there's rot festering somewhere

in the bowels of this room;

// i can feel it //

it coats the back of my teeth with brackish mold.

// sinks to the pulp //

The figures sit, a scaffolding of bones and heat and sinew; desperately, tragically human. The

woman who's only part woman holds her hands out like first communion. She trembles. The

other doesn't even flinch.

VENA CAVA

Here's the dark of blood; here's the webbing of veins, just under the skin. Yearning like a baring

of arteries.

UNKNOWN (V.O)

i can feel myself beginning to unravel—

head disconnecting from the rest of my body,

a voyeur peering down into the

soft spot behind my clavicle.

waiting.

bracing for the un-wanting to find its mark;

to burrow into the crevices, where

every augury of exodus has already

taken root in my mind.

The air is now opaque with shadows that stretch across the room like spider silk.

The shapes in the corner spit blood.

UNKNOWN (V.O)

is this how you thought it'd play out?

you said you wanted to hear it all.

you wanted to know.

i guess this is what i wanted too,

deep down.

after all, don't say you love me

unless you really mean it;

unless you've seen every facet of my mind —

turned it around and around in the light.

when i vomit shades of depression

like an exorcism across the tile;

when i empty the static from my brain onto the dinner table,

will you still want me?

CORNEA

We see the two figures, still seated on the kitchen flood. They never break eye contact. Neither

one is holy. The shadows eat them whole.

UNKNOWN (V.O.)

can you love me in spite of it all?

FADE OUT.

THE END

tinderbox

you're kissing me in the backseat of a burning car

     and i'm trying to tell you that the fire's

          scorching my dress.

but you just trail your scathing mouth down the length of my throat—

     a ghosting of smoke.

you watch me turn to ash in your hands.

               you don't even wince.

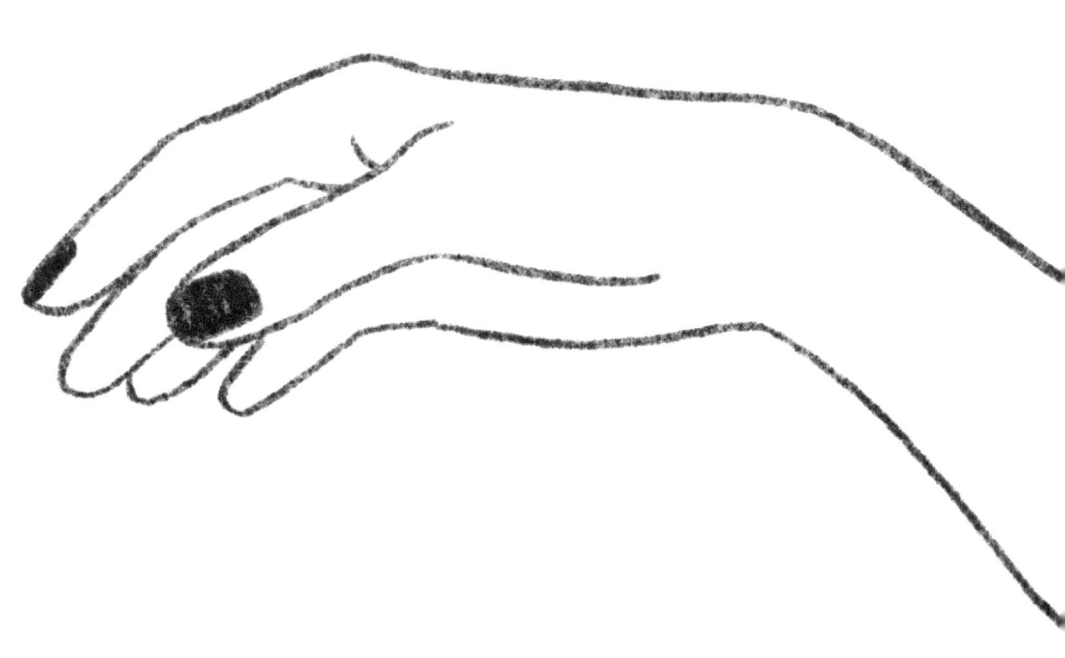

ACT TWO

bisection

i wanted nothing more

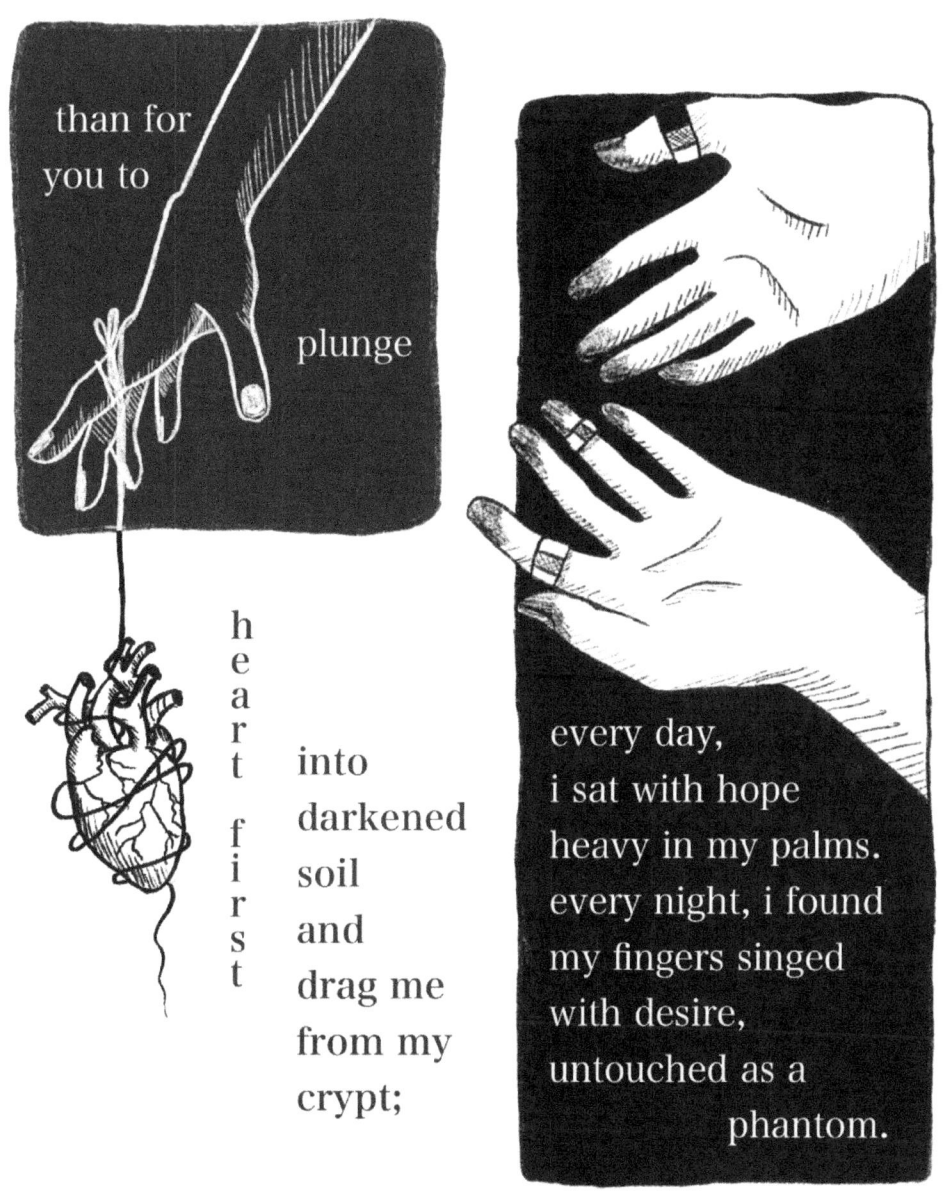

than for
you to

plunge

h
e
a
r
t

f
i
r
s
t

into
darkened
soil
and
drag me
from my
crypt;

every day,
i sat with hope
heavy in my palms.
every night, i found
my fingers singed
with desire,
untouched as a
            phantom.

i should have known —
        you were never one to get
your hands dirty.

two am fatalism

i loved you in that hand-trembling,

breath-like-a-bird-in-the-back-of-your-throat kind of way.

the kind of way that makes your skin shimmer and ache with hunger.

even now, you speak

and my ribs splinter apart with longing.

from the beginning, i knew it wouldn't work.

hell, it wouldn't even get a chance to start.

    // my hands were too clumsy, and your heart was underripe //

so i sat and rotted for you—

                                    decomposition in stasis.

it's the way i embrace self-destruction

like a body falling from a twelve-story building.

    i used to tell myself that if i just suffered

tragically // elegantly // interestingly enough—

    if i vomited up carnations instead of sickness—

    then maybe you could love me // maybe you could find me palatable.

self-annihilation was never the goal,

but it just looked so goddamn appealing if it meant you might tolerate me in your life.

but holding fast to the blade that has only ever hollowed you out,

wasted you to bonemeal, is not devotion.

it's throwing yourself on a spike

and hoping your innards look pretty enough to warrant keeping.

so teach me to unlove,

to hide my adoration away in the shallow grave of my chest.

teach me to escape your orbit; to reach terminal velocity.

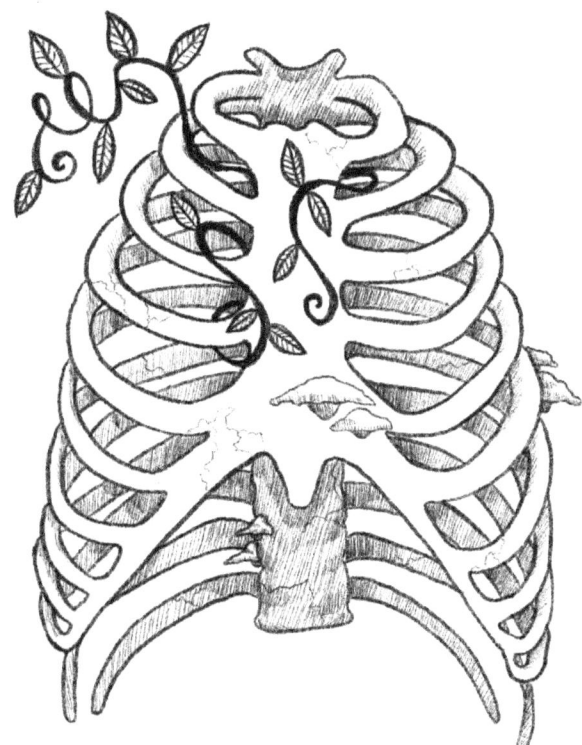

to stop

extending my hand into the growing night and finding

nothing

but

void.

ephemeral

i dreamt about you again last night. i don't remember much;

i think i'm forgetting what you look like.

when i'm awake, you're just a blur of heat and breath

and eyes dark as the salt-breathed sea—a girl deified under a silver moon.

       // even in the time before, you were always more gossamer than flesh //

yet somehow in sleep, my mind inverts the mirrors,

pulls back the curtain of smoke.

and then, there you are; warm and solid and real in the space beside me.

and for just a moment, it's as though nothing has changed.

autoclave / 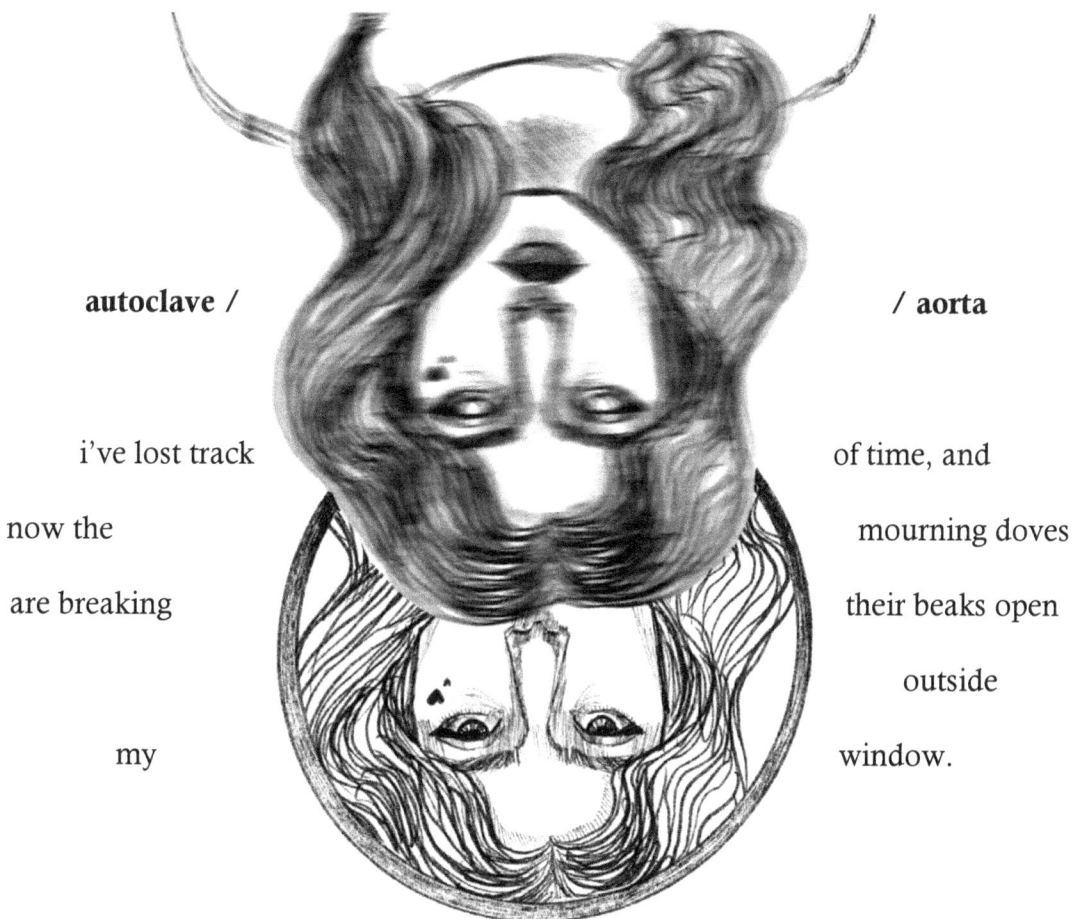 **/ aorta**

i've lost track of time, and

now the mourning doves

are breaking their beaks open

outside

my window.

i've spent the night coaxing every last remnant of love from under my sternum,

scrubbing muscle down to bone.

i've unpicked all the arteries, unstrung the nerves and gristle,

and cauterized every last memory of breath that ever spoke your name aloud.

and i think i'm getting better, i truly do.

but know that if you came to me in forty years time,

when my hair is streaked silver and wild,

when you have lines that run rivulets down your cheeks

   —if you kissed my eyelids and begged me for me back—

i would open the door wide as a wound.

i would set the table with my best silver, knives polished to execution

(an abattoir of mahogany and my aunt's best tablecloth).

here, on this altar place,

i'll serve my still-thrashing heart,

raging cardinal in the bone china of my breastbone.

'cause here's the thing. / there's a bracing, terrible part of me that worries i'll never get over you / i'm terrified that i'm going to roll over and find someone else keeping your side of the bed warm / that a lover who is not you and never will be / is going to reach for my hand and i'll think of nothing but the birthmark on your palm / i'm afraid that i'll be sitting at dinner / and i'll open the confession box gore of my mouth / and decades of aching and half-realized grief will tumble out onto my plate / [spit the (in)articulation of your absence like fruit seeds] / i'm afraid i'll feel the ghosting of your breath on my skin / and be rendered electric with desire i can never set down.

rageborne

there's a space somewhere in the tangle of my veins where

rage and   love exist in equal measure.

holding your memory in the birdcage of my chest

(the eighth wonder of the world),

ivy sprouts baneful from behind my clavicle,

an unkindness of ravens // an itching for retribution.

if you're careful,

     and if you look close enough,

you can find raspberries that bloom overripe and too-sweet;

a tenderness that threatens to consume me whole.

believe me, if i could uproot them both—bury a weeding knife deep into the gritted

pith of my core and pull it all out, brambled and moldering as a ravine—i would.

but invasive species have always been so hard to kill,

     and i'm not one to be cruel.

knife me in two and watch me bleed absence

there's a set of knives on top of the fridge that just

        sit there;

that hold a gaze of their own like a sentient, breathing thing.

        what i'm trying to say is that i'm all

        irregular teeth and plunging-cliffside-nose.

        i'm all bones arranged strangely under the skin

        and too much waist

        and not enough hip

        and too much shoulder

        and not enough chest

    and what i'm trying to say is that

        i think about kitchen knives (a lot).

i think about using them to pare myself down into something more

    appetizing.

(look, i can sit pretty if you promise you'll still want me after dinner's done and the dishes have

all been put away).

what i'm trying to say

       is that i waste my circadian rhythm

       to its frazzled ends, break my sanity

       on the sharpened edge of my fingernails;

         the insatiable need for perfection—

         to excavate every pore, turn them all lesioned and oozing.

       because so long as i can control the destruction,

         so long as the hurt cleaves open by my own hand,

i can pretend i'm the captain of this rusted ship, the one championing the chariot;

       i can pretend i'm in control.

but how do you stop the guilt that comes simply from existing?

how do you learn to inhabit a body you've been taught to hate?

ambivalence

i'd like to believe that i'm a good friend; / that a lifetime of begging to be made useful is enough. / but i constantly find myself being too much / or nothing at all. / 'cause i'm either caring too deeply, / too frantically / (the desperate frenzy to be loved) / or canceling all my plans to rot away in my room, / apathy like saprotroph. / i cannibalize my potential. / i tear myself to shreds, if only to feel like a good person / —if only to justify existence.

i don't know. maybe i'm just looking for new ways to self-destruct.

novocain grief

i don't know if my body has ever truly learned the contours of grief.

every trauma, every loss and eroded casualty that comes with existence

      remains hoarded in the recesses of a desperate mind.

but a brain half-drowning in denial can only go so far

      before the dam breaks and the river runs thick with

         blood.

how long can this sorrow stay submerged?

        (how much longer

                can i hold my breath?)

20 february 2020

everything feels a little hellish right now.
~like i'm full up with gasoline and only
a match's width away from ~~total~~ annhilatation.

i keep having that fantasy; the one where
the car jumps the curb and i'm there
to catch it.
   i've stopping looking both ways before
crossing the street. i don't know if that
makes me a bad person. ~~i don't know if i
care anymore.~~

i spent an hour and a half last night digging
~~rot from my molars. i wish i could dig
this thing out from under~~
~~i've harbored this feeling out~~
~~i think i've purified~~
~~a corpse and rotting and halting
around with a pulse that just won't quit.~~
~~maybe all my insides have liquified.~~ ~~just a
mass of bile and seeping blood held together
by a husk of skin.~~
   ~~i'm pretty sure spiders liquify the flies trapped
in their webs before they eat them. i also
think caterpillars do that in their~~
chrysalides before they hatch or metamorphize
or whatever.
   suffice to say i don't think i'm the caterpillar

waves

i finish the day in one piece.

i try not to think too hard

        about the railing of the bridge—

             the way it splinters under my grip,

the way it would only take one good shove to topple it

      (to pitch forward //

      to collide with the breakers //

         and purify against the rocks below).

there's nothing romantic about broken skin

if you're going to tell me ocd is a blessing.

    that you'd love to be neat and tidy,

i'm going to show you every inch of cracked and broken skin on my body,

    and the way i've rubbed my hands bloody with soap.

    // that time i drank hydrogen peroxide because i swear i could feel the virus squirming

around in my gut like something insidious //

    i will show you every shirt i've bleached orange with fear,

every hour i've spent researching illness and goodness and the cataclysmic shuddering "what if"

that lurks like a predator

in every corner of every room.

tell me, "everyone is a little ocd",

and i'll show you every light switched off;

// and on and off and on and off ad infinitum //

    every word repeated under my breath like some apocalyptic ritual until i'm

hoarse and sobbing.

    because a broken chain of events // a misplaced thought // a misplaced step, and the people i love disintegrate like ash in my mind,

terror burning a hole in my cheek.

i carry names and numbers and every reassuring mantra in my mouth like embers

    because there's a knife behind my eyes and my mind tells me i'm the only one who can

stop the fall of the blade.

tell me, is it romantic how my room hasn't been cleaned in months

    because the thing living inside me

        // the thing that grips my amygdala like a vise //

    tells me that it's unsafe, that it's too much

        too much

            too much // always too much //?

so you can try to glamourize the tears of frustration,

    idealize the relentless tick-tick-ticking of a brain that can't // that won't //

            stop.

      dress me up in frills and call me "quirky", and as long as i hide the

compulsions well enough,

        you can pretend it's not really there.

yeah, you can romanticize it all you want,

but i think you'd be better off not.

scaling the good // taming the rot

god like a panopticon

plucking aorta from host

　　　　　　// heavy as heat //.

am i unsightly?

　　　　　　　　　　　　// am i unearthly? //

can i scrape virtue from the roof of my mouth and balance the scales?

　　bile like ichorous (pronounced "icarus" with a mouthful of wax),

　　weights like an un/fluttering of wings.

rearranging vertebrae,

digging rot from cavities of marrow.

　　　　// pull dendrite from axon and audit the contents of my brain //

am i good?

am i (good) enough to warrant this life that is not my own;

// a great borrowing of atoms //

　　this life that might be better served with another soul inhabiting its walls?

self-made slaughter

there's this vacuous dark tugging unease from deep in my core. and i'm nearly twenty-one,

but i'm still cutting my teeth on the edge of a tombstone.

when the doctor asks me if i've had any thoughts of   self-harm,

i roll my shoulder in its socket.

// a site of violence—the place where i've spent long nights turning myself into a

                        slaughterhouse //

i hesitate before telling her i've never felt better,

      a grin pressed into my skin   like the serration of a blade.

what i think i'm trying to tell you is that i almost didn't make it,

and i know everyone thinks it's the hormones

          (they swear on it),

but on my seventeenth birthday i thought about getting out,

about picking myself up off the floor and walking

     headlong into traffic.

     about capsizing, secluded, slow slow slow into the lake by my house.

     an unblemished expanse of water

     like an amniotic sac

        (aphrodite unbirthed and screaming).

what i think i'm trying to say is that i spent my adolescence dry heaving into cracked and

burning fields / unseating the sky with rage / sinking wisdom teeth into anything that would

have me / ungutting myself and pretending the stitches make me whole.

    and what i think i'm trying to say is that

    i haven't been able to feel anything for so long that i'm half-convinced my

neurons have calcified.

    maybe my brain is already practicing death like a conjuring trick.

    maybe i putrefied the year i turned thirteen;

    a corpse exhumed and lurching around

    with a pulse that just won't quit.

        // a body full up of graveyard dirt—a necropolis quarried from

      between ligaments //

                                            but i'm getting better, i think.

    this morning, i woke up with light slanting across my cheek and for the first time

in a long time, i felt the blood hushing under my skin and

didn't beg for it to   stop,   to find a way out of my body and onto the

    floor.

evading the feast

i am sixteen and a man i don't know leers at me out the window of his truck.

    malice froths in the corners of his lips as he tells me how much of a

    dirty bitch i am, how he'd like to

        fuck me from behind.

and just like that, my heart scuttles into my windpipe, choking me half-dead with fear.

    and like every woman i've ever met,

        i was born with keys erupting from between my fingers and an apology

        already rotting in my throat.

        i carry a river rock in my pocket wherever i go

        —hold it like a shield at my side.

i want to make this man feel as terrified as i do, set his hands trembling and stomach

swirling, oil-soaked and desecrated with fear.

        but his teeth are too sharp, and my fists are too small, so i sprint home, veins

        webbed crimson with every electric pulse of adrenaline.

i am sixteen and i am a slab of meat, a thing to be salivated over

    —slippery tongues sliding over incisors like a glistening, wet beast all its own.

here, i'm nothing more than

    a flayed pig hanging in the window of a butchery

// jugular vein held open for slaughter //

i exist only when their roving eyes seek to undress me.

so, i am sixteen

and i make a vanishing act of myself. hips, waist, shoulders heavy like the succubus they

tell me i am, slipping below the cover of my father's oversized sweaters. i hide the heat of my

skin, the shape of my body—praying i won't whet the appetites of greedy, gnashing mouths

(though we both know a cardigan never saved anyone).

i am sixteen and the world has jagged edges. and i haven't

learned to throw a punch yet,

how to line my stomach with teeth and corrugate

the back of my throat with thorns so that every time i speak,

i am taken seriously.

but *i am sixteen*

and i am trying.

maneater

it's the heat behind my mother's eyes that crackles like a wildfire.

it's the way she says "be back before dark", as if praying to some omnipotent god;

    as though if i can just cling to the bright edge of daylight for a little longer

        —if i can outrun the night—

    then i'll be allowed to return intact

          (as if sunlight has been anything more than a false savior).

but we're born with canines serrated like daggers and buried under our tongues like a secret.

    so when they make monsters of us

    // too loud, too big, too *tempting* // we sharpen our teeth and

        bite back.

if they deny us a soft existence,

we'll spit venom and take it by force.

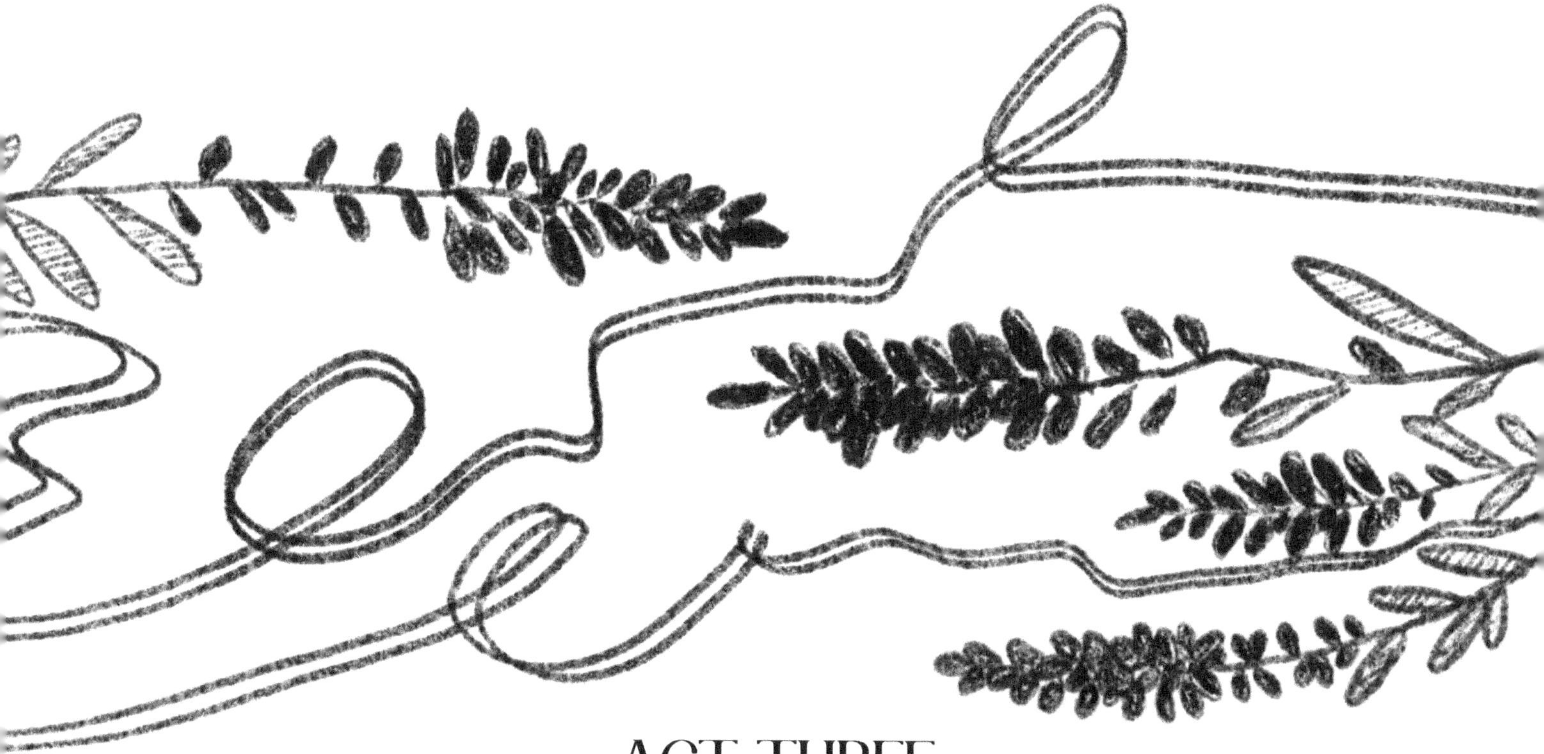

ACT THREE

unloving the knife

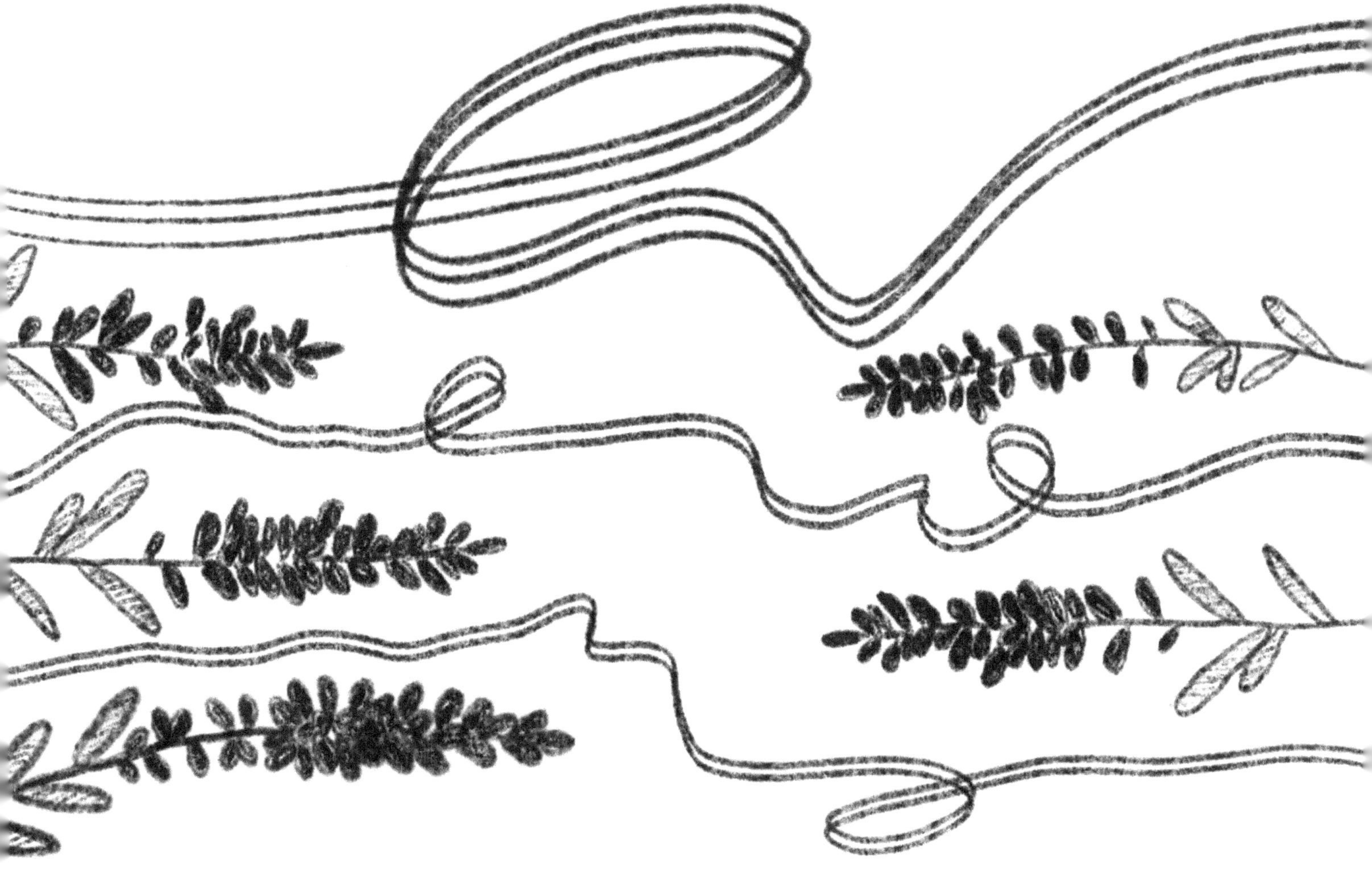

rebirth

here is the unbuckling of knees,

the unwriting of eulogies.

here is rebirth;

embryonic plasma and placenta like a bitter thing.

here is the unbowing from tombs.

welcome to the final act.

this is the part where i play the miracle—

    the thing raking itself   from the soil.

i'm alive

and doing oh so much more than just kicking.

-    fuck you

building the house haunted

i wish you the best, truly, i do.

but i'd be lying if i said there isn't a small spiteful part of me

that burns caustic through the lining of my stomach—

a part of me that hopes i fucking haunt you.

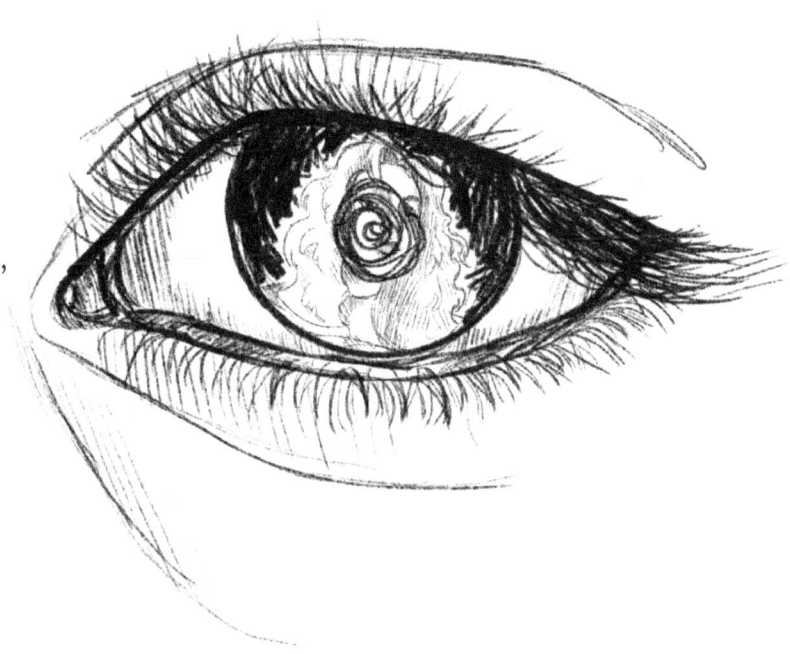

that every time you close your eyes,

i am the imprint on the dark on your cornea,

floating heavy in the pool of your iris.

// some graveless apparition //

here's the grey lady

        clawing herself dripping and half-drowned from the lake.

here's every dream

        teeming with the silhouette of my shape,

a sensation of remembrance; a saturation of scent—

teeth gnawing wretched and raw at the pulp of your subconscious.

artemis // bladed woman

in the prickling dark of october,

    a girl is born bright and clotted under the red of a still-bleeding moon.

when she rises (as every overlooked thing inevitably does),

she stains the night vicious with her wrath.

      we all know the way teeth slide into slippery flesh,

      the way a woman wronged will unhinge her jaw to devour the ocean,

      the way she'll pull salt from the earth into pillars,

      crystalline and aortic and thrashing

      (the solar gravity of rage).

so when arrows erupt from the back of her throat,

and blades line the tip of her tongue,

she walks alone

through the shadow-steeped night;

she spits knives at cruel men.

autonomy in the age of greed

when was the last time you felt complete ownership of your own bones?

your body in its entirety, unburdened by roving, hungry eyes?

i want to be gruesome.

ophelia, eroticized even in death, here now she rises, rebirthed from the water and

screaming. here's the burning witch dragging herself from the stake, all chainsaw-jaw

and chestful of god. here's a woman with storms under her skin, crackling and hissing

"fuck you" like an

incantation. my mother passes quiet fury down like an inheritance, and we sit

with it like a heavy weight in our guts, trade knowing glances over dinner. My

sister presses her knife a little harder against her plate, grinds her teeth, and

bites back a scream. my best friend spits it out in bits and pieces—sparrow

bones, bullets of grief.

("domesticate your rage. make it appetizing")

i pour another glass of tepid water.

i sweep resentment off the edge of the dinner table like breadcrumbs.

indelible

don't try to edit me out of the narrative;

      it was never yours to (re)write,

      you were never the one in charge.

see, the funny thing is,

when you spend a year and a half with love

      bladed and pressed in between your ribs,

it tends to leave a mark.

even now, my hands open like the doors of a crypt,

my palms tattooed over with your name.

and i'm here, the lady incarnate,

scrubbing &

    scrubbing &

      scrubbing until my flesh unfurls like butterfly wings under foaming soap.

so how *dare* you pretend none of this ever happened,

    lock me out and call me crazy for knocking on the front door

    when we both know i'm the one who built the goddamned house.

you can't erase me—

i am both the reckoning and the mourning.

i am the impression of light

that holds your vision long after the fire has gone out.

i stand here, broken and bitter as i am—

living proof that whoever said

"absence makes the heart grow fonder"

was a fucking liar.

when i say "i hate you" with a mouthful of razors,

know that i won't let you forget me

until the stars burn themselves to extinction

and the planets crumble to devastation.

i am the hum in your chest,
the grit in your teeth,

and i refuse to be confined
to the mildness of your
memory.

bite back

i've spent so long carrying this body like an offering plate,

begging to be devoured—not caring if they spit me out when they're done.

so long as i'm carved wide with teeth marks,

i know i am wanted.

the shape of the craving is inconsequential:

both the hunted deer and looming god are pursued with a hunger that shakes the sky.

i've unmade and rebirthed myself a thousand times over

trying to love you the way you want to be loved.

        i set myself alight, and you complain about the heat.

        i freeze my blood cold, but you hate the way the snow falls.

        i exist lukewarm and barely breathing,

        and you're just so bored of me.

it's taken me too long to realize that i don't have to whittle

myself down to the pit

just because you gave me the time of day every other week.

// just because you wanted to feel full in the wake of my emptiness //

but make no mistake; these are my lungs,

    my hands.

my mouth,

my skin.

my body.   and it is not to be used as kindling

just so you can critique the way the fire   burns.

i am mine,

          and i will *never*

be yours

    again.

sutures

i would have kissed you if you'd asked.

    (hell, i think

i would've ripped my lungs clean from my chest if that's what it took).

turn the tapes forward, and now

    it's been a year and a half of radio silence and

    there's still blood staining my gums—

      still acid curdling under my tongue.

i'm not that same little girl
who once loved you.

but i've ripped myself jagged, sharpened the angles, and pieced myself back together—

    saved myself when the knight in shining armor stood me up at the gate.

i'm not that same little girl who once stitched her heart to your hands,

and believe me when i say, she's never coming back.

dottie

if matter cannot be created or destroyed,

then isn't it true that i haven't lost you at all?

       at least not in your entirety.

perhaps you've altered your shape a little,

condensing into shadows and outlines i don't yet recognize or understand.

       but when you sink into the cool green of the earth

       and let the soil drink the marrow from your bones,

       are you not the same clover that brushes my ankles;

       the same birch trees that kiss the sky vermillion?

and maybe your body is gone and i'm left behind,

    this grief like an inheritance.

and maybe i'll never hear your voice calling from the other room // watch your eyes light

on the dawn.

but you live on in the rain and the light and every

warm soft thing that grows in the sun.

so i break a little less each day; i reach to hold hands with the shadows that once held

your form.

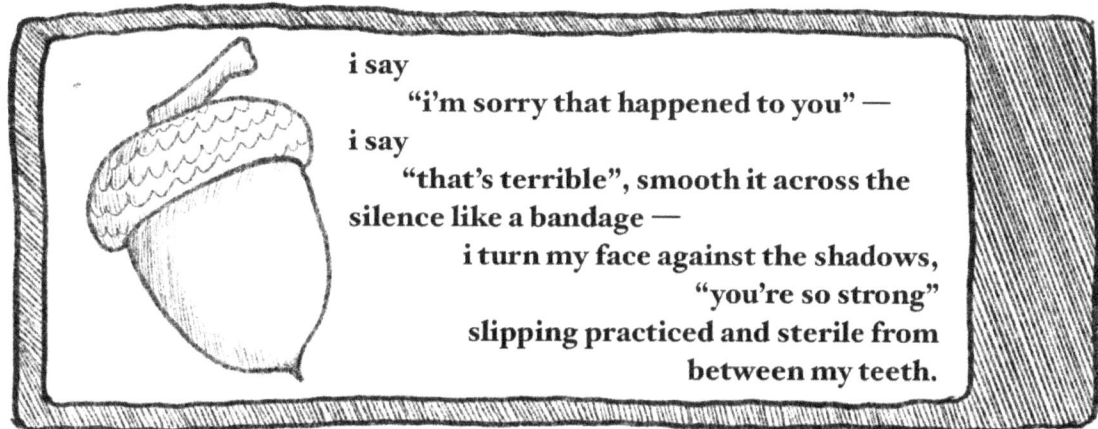

i say
    "i'm sorry that happened to you" —
i say
    "that's terrible", smooth it across the
silence like a bandage —
    i turn my face against the shadows,
        "you're so strong"
slipping practiced and sterile from
    between my teeth.

and i swallow all the rest like coedine syrup. i bite my tongue in two.

because you deserve so much more than these mangled, half-acknowledgements

        of tragedy.

instead, i want to tell you that you don't deserve any of this. that i know you know this already, but none of this was your fault. that you might not have the strength to claw your way out of bed right now and that's alright; that there's no timer counting down until the moment when you're meant to be

okay.

dragging yourself clear of the wreckage is anything but romantic.

you are a good person, and i'll stay here as the wounds begin to unache (i know they might never fully disappear, and that's okay). i'll be here, kneeling on the floor by your pillow, feeding you warmth and clutching your hand like an anchor.

and i'm sorry this happened to you (is happening to you now)

and i'm sorry the world just keeps spinning as though everything's fine —
as though you're not staggering to keep pace.

and i wish i could take this all away,

could undo every wretched thing you've endured —
    pull every knife from your back, stitch every wound and fade every scar.

but this isn't my story to write.

so i'll be here,

// heart in hand //

if you need me.

spring cleaning: a spell

find a stone the size of your fist,

sharp and stratified as your bladed palm.

the lines of your hands tell a story.

              maybe it's one you'd prefer to forget.

but the grooves of your skin

weave the tapestry of every gentle thing

you've ever touched (every brutal thing that's touched you).

there's an aching that pitches out of your open mouth,

a fear that sears your outline and burrows deep into the ends of your hair.

           but, love, you are so much more than what's had the audacity to hurt you.

so write every miserable, devastating thing on the stone.

bury it somewhere deep and dark and green;

the ground will hold your anger like a secret.

wash your hands in running water.

we will be here when you return   like a great harkening of storm clouds,

all crackling light and ruthless sky.

lightedlove

be gentle with yourself, my love.

you are a brain inhabiting a body that seeks only to love you to ~~death~~ life.

if you were to unstitch every nerve ending, every muscle fiber,

you would find the most vibrant warmth,

glistening gold

        in the lightning   heat.

it's summertime and we're all bleeding ichor,

so when you press your fingertips

to the slope of your temples,

think reverence.

        think hands folded in worship.

you are holy and unbreaking;

        a church of flesh and bone.

you are so much more than they would have you believe—

a forest fire made manifest,

the ocean that towers high overhead and

$\qquad\qquad\qquad$ breaks

$\quad$ like vengeance on the rocks.

and yet here you are,

walking around as though you're not the closest thing to god.

unloving the knife

i've always told myself that if i could just make myself smaller, more digestible;

if i could apologize for taking up space,

      for living in a body made of irregular shapes,

             // this anarchy of flesh //

          then maybe i could be worthy of love.

but i often fail to remember that these are

      the same legs

          that carried my great-grandmother through the depression;

      the same shoulders

          that stoked kindling to fuel the fire in my mother's belly

        and her's before her.

because every woman i've ever met has a quiet rage

that burns red hot in her gut like

            the pulse of god.

   (think prometheus // think burning).

and i, in my girl-like state,

hold that same fire like a promise.

i am renaissance-faced and unflinching,

carrying the image of all the ones that came before—

                a legacy of witches and healers, of farmers and sharp-tongued daughters;

                              all aquailine angles.

                        // eyes brazen and unrelenting //

and believe me when i say

there are still days when i want to slice the smooth muscle

from my face and eat it raw so i don't have to look at myself anymore.

but more days than not,

      when i gaze into a mirror,

i see every iteration of this

         strange, lovely body

staring back at me;

refracting through time and space—

        generations of women unspooling in a never-ending line.

                        because it's always too big,

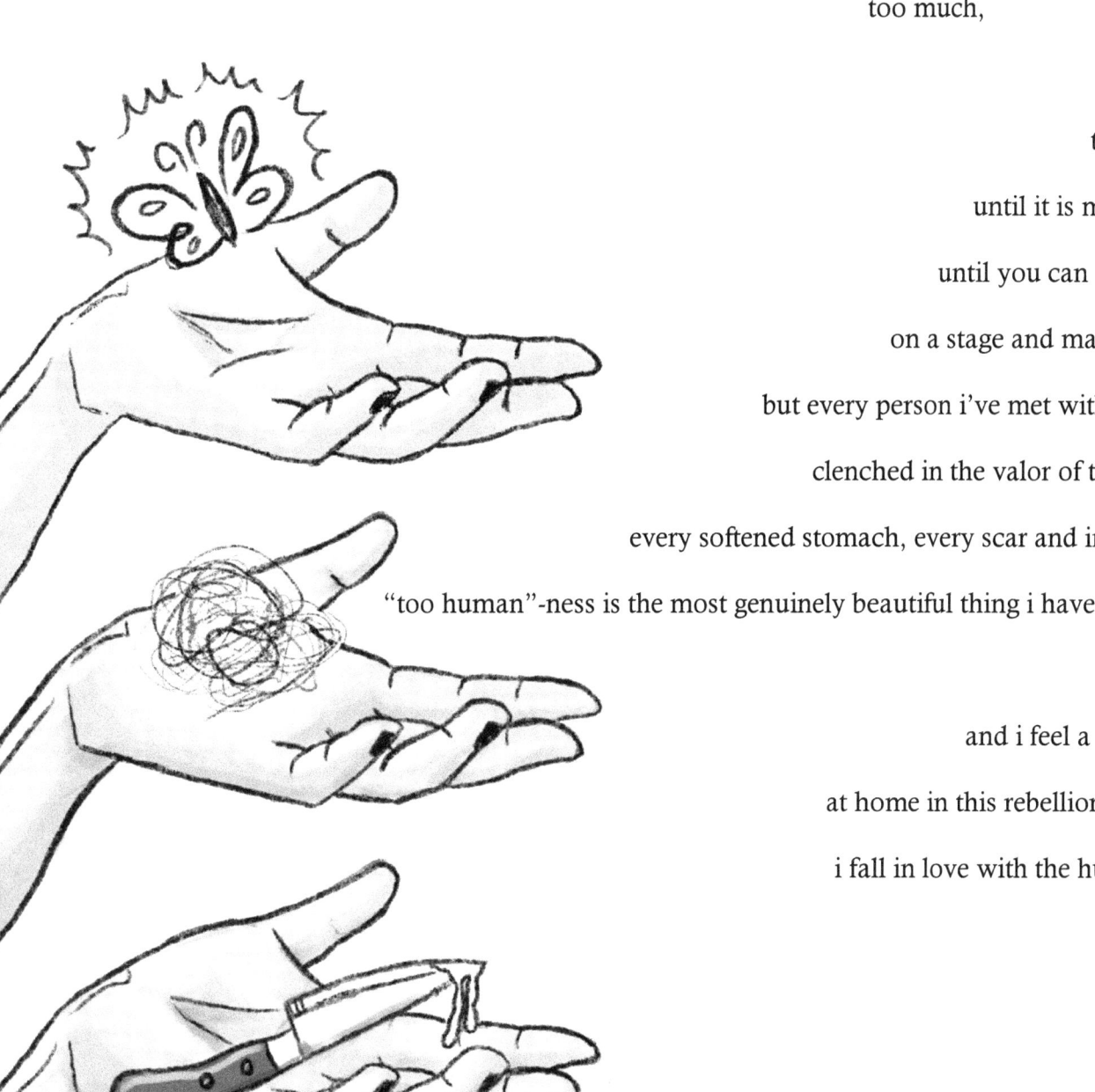

too much,   too little,

too heavy

too human

until it is marketable.

until you can stand it up

on a stage and make it walk.

but every person i've met with kindness

clenched in the valor of their jaw—

every softened stomach, every scar and inch of that

"too human"-ness is the most genuinely beautiful thing i have ever seen.

and i feel a little more

at home in this rebellion of bones;

i fall in love with the humanness.

mental health & crisis intervention resources

- national suicide prevention lifeline (united states): 1-800-273-talk (8255)
  - the trevor lifeline (united states): 1-866-488-7386
  - the crisis textline (united states): text "home" to 741-741
  - trans lifeline (united states & canada): 1-877m-565-8860
  - canada suicide prevention service (canada): 1-833-456-4566
  - kids help phone (canada): 1-800-668-6868
- hope for wellness help line (specifically for Indigenous peoples in so-called Canada who require crisis aid/counseling): 1-855-242-3310
  - assaulted women's helpline (toronto) — 1-866-863-0511
- support services for male survivors of sexual abuse program (ontario) — 1-866-887-0015
  - toronto distress centres — 1-416-408-4357
  - multilingual distress line (ontario) — 1-905-459-7777
  - lgbt youthline (canada) — 1-800-268-9688
  - saptel (méxico) - 55-5259-812
- instituto nacional de psiquiatria (méxico): 55-5655-3080 o 1-800-953-1704